Little Otis Fights Cancer
A True Story
By Otis Keith

Published by Love is You

Illustrated by Richa Kinra Arts

Published by Love is You
Illustrations by Richa Kinra Arts

Manufactured in the United States.

ISBN: 978-0-578-13892-3

My name is Otis. I am 6 years old.
I like going to school.

One day I did not feel good.
My side hurt.

I told my mother. She thought I didn't want to go to school, so she decided to take me to the doctor.

The doctor said I have to go right to Children's Hospital where I was admitted. My parents were told I had cancer of the kidney.

I was put in a room with two other little kids, Timothy and Samantha. We would play together when we were allowed to get out of bed or when we were not feeling sick.

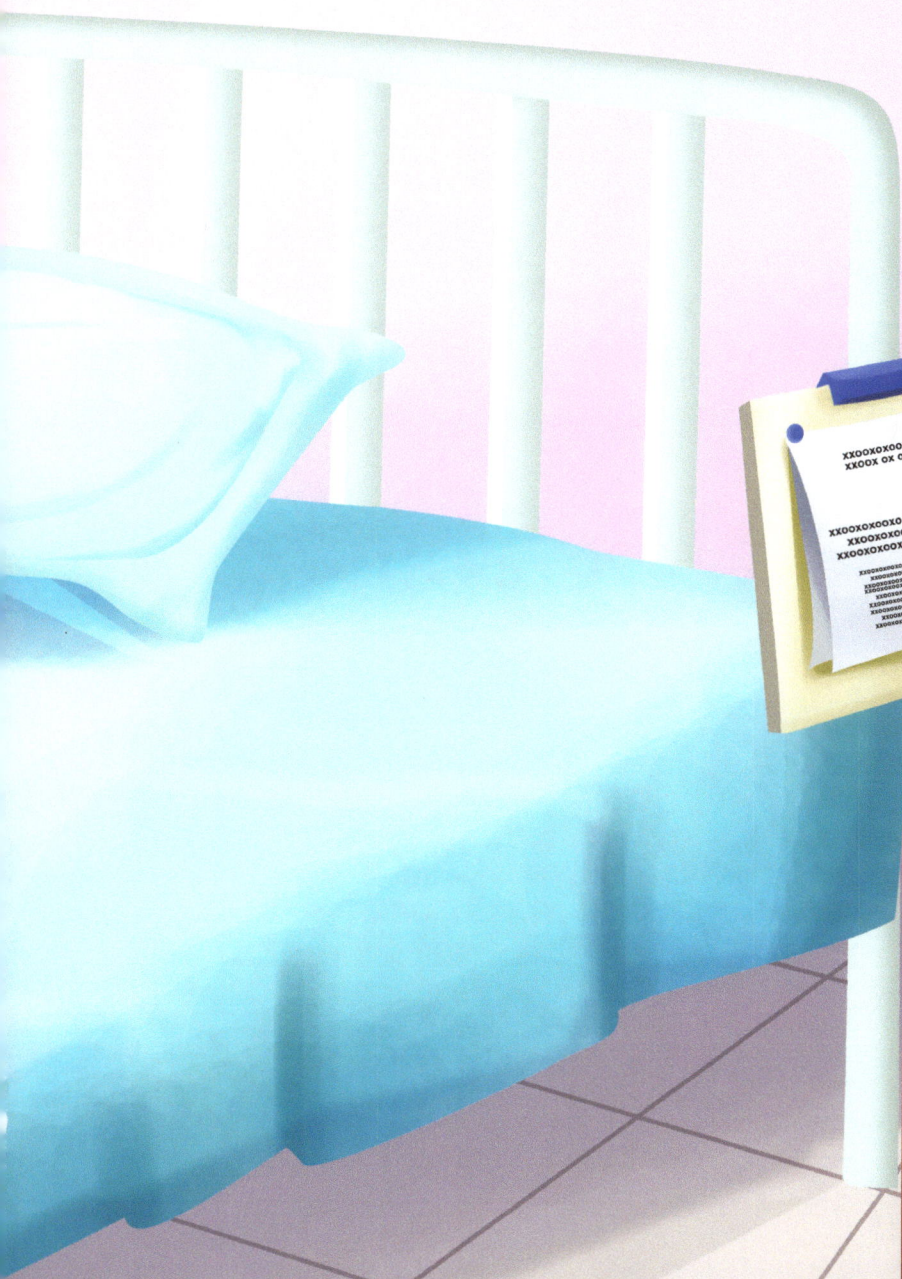

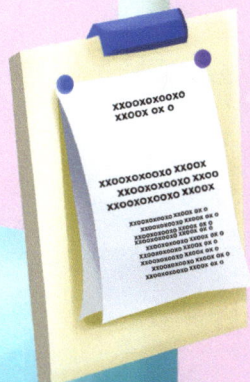

When I was feeling sick I didn't want to eat the hospital food. My favorite food was a banana sandwich, and the nurses would make it for me and it made me feel better.

I had to have lots of radiation before I could have surgery. It made me sick. Then I had my surgery and started chemo, and it made me sicker.

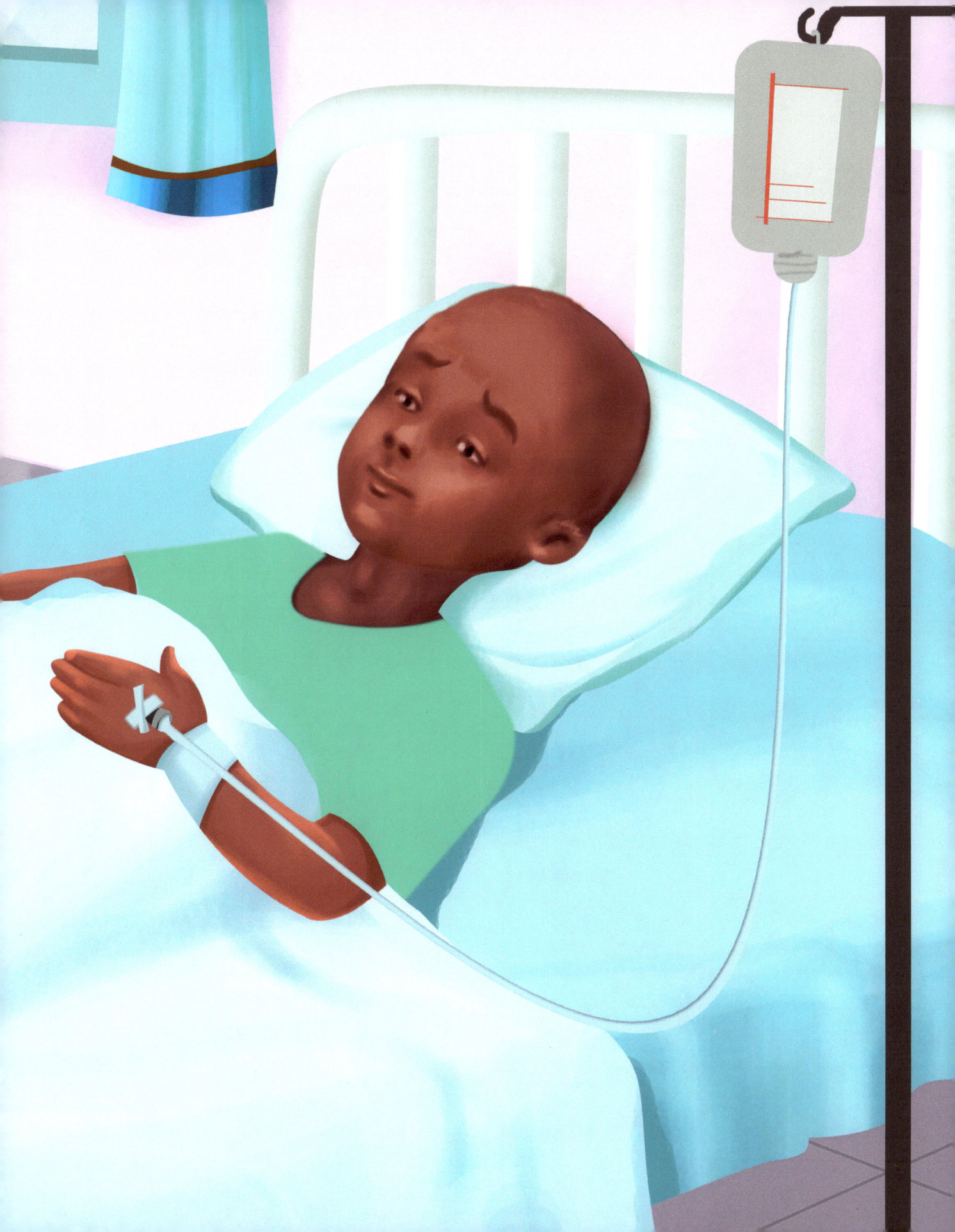

The chemo made my hair fall out. I felt kind of bad about it but I was glad to be home. Time went by and then when I went back to Children's Hospital for a follow up treatment and we got bad news.

My parents were told I had cancer again. It was now in my lungs. So back in the hospital I went. I had another surgery and started chemo again. My mom would take me to my second home, the hospital, twice a week.

It seems like I was on chemo for years, but I finally stopped and my hair grew back. I was so happy. I lived like a normal child.

I love to sing and one day I'm going to be a singing star.

Thanks to Children's Hospital I grew up like my mom and dad and started my own family with a wife, kids and grandkids and you will to.

With good doctors and family
support and God all in my
corner, I fought a good fight, and
I beat cancer.
Now I'm in my 50's.

The End

www.ingramcontent.com/pod-product-compliance
Lightning Source LLC
LaVergne TN
LVHW072133070426
835513LV00002B/93